CV

RAIN FORESTS

LUSH TROPICAL PARADISE

JENNY WOOD

Gareth Stevens Children's Books
MILWAUKEE

Wonderworks of Nature:

Caves: An Underground Wonderland
Coral Reefs: Hidden Colonies of the Sea
Deserts: An Arid Wilderness
Icebergs: Titans of the Oceans
Rain Forests: Lush Tropical Paradise
Storms: Nature's Fury
Volcanoes: Fire from Below
Waterfalls: Nature's Thundering Splendor

For a free color catalog describing Gareth Stevens' list of high-quality children's books, call 1-800-341-3569 (USA) or 1-800-461-9120 (Canada).

Picture Credits:
Ardea — 5, 8 (top); Bruce Coleman — 8 (bottom), 9 (top), 12 (both); Mark Edwards — 23; Hutchinson — 13, 16, 18, 19; Frank Lane — 10 (both), 14 (both), 15 (both); Nature Photographs — back cover; Oxford Scientific Films — 20; Planet Earth Pictures — 22; Tony Stone — front cover; Survival Anglia — 9 (bottom), 11, 17 (both)

Illustration Credits:
All illustrations by Francis Mosley except pp. 24-28, Jon Davis/Linden Artists
Line art: Keith Ward

Library of Congress Cataloging-in-Publication Data

Wood, Jenny.
    Rain forests : lush tropical paradise / Jenny Wood. — North American ed.
        p.   cm. — (Wonderworks of nature)
    First published under title: Jungles.
    Includes index.
    Summary: Discusses the tropical rain forests of the world, where they occur, what life they support, and how they are being threatened and destroyed.
    ISBN 0-8368-0632-8
    1. Rain forest ecology—Juvenile literature. 2. Rain forests—Juvenile literature. [1. Rain forests. 2. Rain forest ecology. 3. Ecology.] I. Wood, Jenny. Jungles. II. Title. III. Series: Wood, Jenny. Wonderworks of nature.
QH541.5.R27W66 1991
508.3152'0913—dc20   91-3786

This North American edition first published in 1991 by
Gareth Stevens Children's Books
1555 North RiverCenter Drive, Suite 201
Milwaukee, Wisconsin 53212, USA

This U.S. edition copyright © 1991. First published in the United Kingdom by Two-Can Publishing, Ltd. Text copyright © 1991 by Jenny Wood.

Printed in the United States of America

2 3 4 5 6 7 8 9 97 96 95 94 93

CONTENTS

All words in **boldface** can be found in the glossary.

WHAT IS A RAIN FOREST?

A tropical rain forest is an area of densely packed trees and plants that lies near the equator, the imaginary line that separates the earth into northern and southern halves, or hemispheres. Rain falls almost every day, and the temperature varies very little between the hottest and the coldest months. Tropical rain forests are packed with all kinds of vegetation, from trees and vines to shrubs and brightly colored flowers. About half the world's **species** of plants and animals live in tropical rain forests.

▶ A tropical rain forest in Australia.

Emergent Layer

Canopy Layer

Understory or 'middle' Layer

Shrub Layer

Forest floor

◀ The layers of vegetation in a tropical rain forest:
Emergent layer: Some trees grow up to 200 feet (61 m) tall.
Canopy layer: Trees in this layer grow from 100 feet (30 m) to 150 feet (46 m) tall. Their tops form a roof of leaves over the forest.
Understory or "middle" layer: Shorter trees growing beneath the canopy form this layer. They reach a height of about 66 feet (20 m).
Shrub layer: This layer has short, woody plants. The tall trees block the sunlight and only a few shrubs are able to grow.
Forest floor: Very little sunlight reaches the forest floor. A thick covering of leaves, twigs, and animal droppings, as well as the remains of dead animals and plants, builds up.

ALL AROUND THE WORLD

Tropical rain forests cover about 7 percent of the earth's surface. They occupy large areas of Central and South America, West Africa, and Asia. Smaller areas are found in Australia and New Guinea. All tropical rain forests have similar characteristics, but different animal and plant species thrive on each of the different continents.

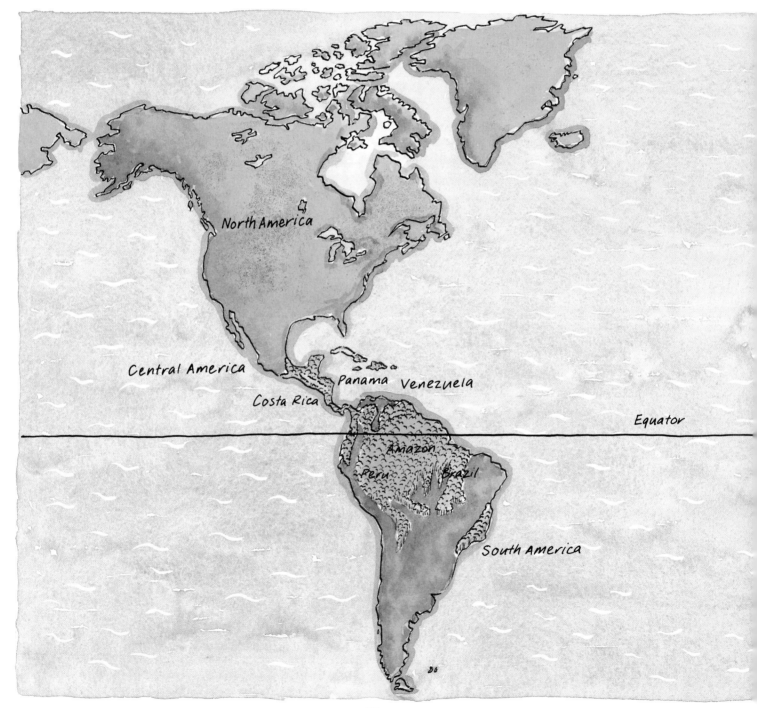

The world's tropical rain forests are in great danger. They are being cut down to provide timber and firewood, and to make room for homes, roads, farms, and factories. Some areas are being cleared to allow the mining of oil and valuable **minerals** such as gold. Scientists estimate that about 42 million acres (17 million ha) of rain forest are destroyed every year. The **habitats** of thousands of species of animals and plants have already vanished. The way of life of many rain forest peoples is also threatened by these changes.

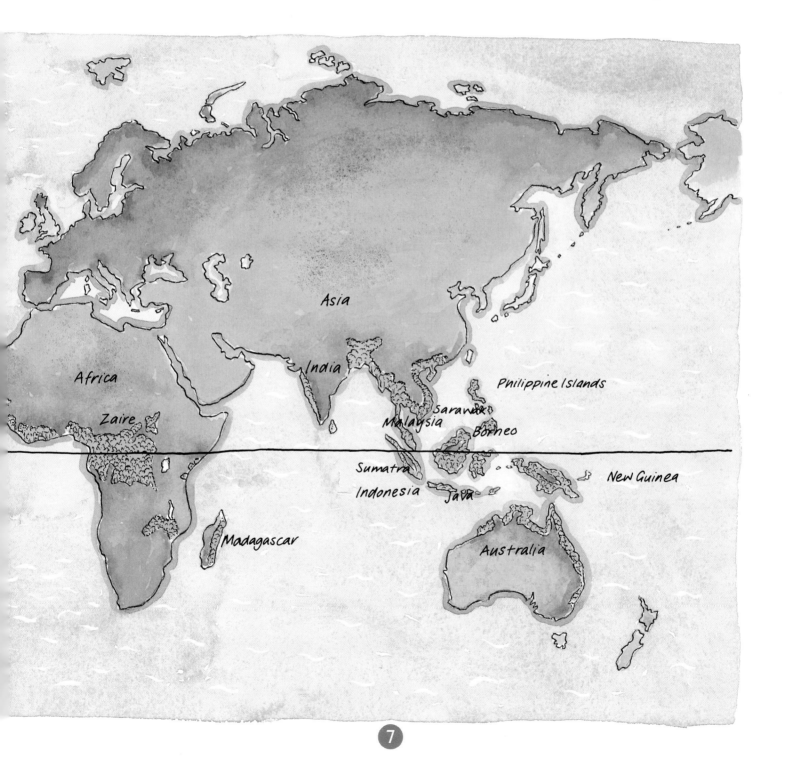

CREEPERS AND CLIMBERS

Trees and plants thrive in the warm, damp conditions of a tropical rain forest. Trees and plants continually bear fruit, and the forest is always green.

Most tropical rain forest trees are **evergreens** that have branches only near the tops of their trunks. The leaves are dark green and tough, with pointed tips to let the rainwater run off. Climbing plants called lianas loop from tree to tree like huge ropes tying the whole forest together. Plants like ferns, mosses, orchids, and **bromeliads** grow on the trunks and branches of living trees.

▲ Rain forests contain many interesting plants. Some of these, such as palms and orchids, have become popular houseplants.

◀ In tropical rain forests, plants known as **epiphytes** grow high on the trees, close to the sunlight. They get food and moisture from the air.

▶ The roots of some tropical rain forest trees form a wide, spreading growth around the tree's base. These buttress roots help keep the tree secure and upright.

◀ The pitcher plant eats insects that are trapped in its tube-shaped leaves. A sweet smell given off by tiny glands inside the top edge of the leaves attracts insects to the plant. When an insect lands, it is trapped by the plant's bristly hairs. It then slides down into the tube.

DID YOU KNOW?

● A tropical rain forest has more tree varieties than any other area of the world. In one section of tropical rain forest in South America, scientists counted 179 different species of trees in an area the size of a large yard.

● About 155,000 of the 250,000 known species of plants are found in tropical rain forests.

● The giant rafflesia produces the largest flowers of any known plant. Unfortunately, the flowers usually smell very unpleasant.

● A scientist at Harvard University has figured out that it would take 25,000 scientists the whole of their working lives to record all the known **flora and fauna** of the world's tropical rain forests.

ROAMING THE RAIN FOREST

Many of the animals in a tropical rain forest spend their lives high in the trees. They have developed remarkable ways of moving through the canopy in search of food such as flowers, leaves, fruit, and nuts. Some, like monkeys and **lemurs**, are very agile and climb well. Others, such as flying squirrels, are able to leap or glide from tree to tree. Snakes loop

▲ Tree frogs eat insects and other small animals. Many can change color to blend in with their surroundings. Some male tree frogs make a high-pitched squeak to attract females. In order to make this sound, the tree frog's throat swells up like a balloon.

▼ The tiger hunts alone, stalking its prey slowly and carefully. It can kill its prey with a single blow of its forepaw.

themselves around branches, while tree frogs have sticky pads on the bottoms of their feet to keep themselves from falling.

Larger animals like antelope, deer, and **tapirs**, as well as small rodents, roam the forest floor. They feed on roots, seeds, leaves, and fruit that falls to the ground. Some animals, such as gorillas, live on the ground as well as in the trees.

Although many tropical rain forest animals are plant-eaters, or herbivores, others, such as jaguars and tigers, are carnivores.

▲ Sloths live in the rain forests of South America and spend most of their time hanging upside down from branches. Their claws grip the branches so securely that they can fall asleep in this position. Sloths often carry their babies on their bellies.

Carnivores hunt and kill other animals for food.

The destruction of so many areas of tropical rain forest means that many animals living there now are in danger of dying out completely. Orangutans, jaguars, and gorillas are some of the rain forest animals threatened with **extinction**.

THE COLORFUL CANOPY

Most tropical rain forest birds live high up in the canopy, where food is plentiful. Hawks and eagles soar above the lush treetops, swooping down from time to time to snatch up other birds, bats, and even monkeys. Many tropical rain forest birds have very brightly colored feathers. Although you might think this would make them easy to spot against the green of the trees, the bright colors really act as a kind of camouflage. The bright spots of color can easily be mistaken for flowers or fruit.

Male bowerbirds, found in the tropical rain forests of New Guinea and Australia, build beautiful bowers, or shelters, in which to court their mates. The bowers are built of grass, moss, twigs, and vines, and are often decorated with brightly colored feathers, berries, shells, and flowers.

► Tropical rain forest birds have developed different ways of feeding. Macaws, for example, use their strong beaks to crack nuts.

◄ Hummingbirds' wings beat so fast that it is almost impossible for the human eye to detect any movement at all. The smallest member of the hummingbird family measures only 2 inches (5 cm) from the tip of its bill to the tip of its tail! Its body is about the same size as that of a large bumblebee, and it weighs less than 0.07 ounces (2 g). Hummingbirds have long, slender bills and long tongues that allow them to suck nectar from the center of even the deepest, tube-shaped flowers.

◄ An African gray parrot enjoys a meal. Like most other types of parrot and macaw, the African gray parrot can hold its food in one foot and bite pieces off, similar to the way humans might eat a sandwich! The parrot keeps its balance by curling its other foot around the branch. A parrot's foot has four toes, two that point to the front, the other two to the back, so it is easy for the bird to grip the branch tightly and securely.

THE TINIEST CREATURES

Scientists believe that up to 80 percent of all the world's insect species live only in tropical rain forests. A recent study of a 2.5-acre (1-ha) area of rain forest in Peru found 41,000 types of insect species living in the canopy alone. There may be between one million and ten million insect species still undiscovered, so if you spent a day collecting insects in a rain forest, you might find a species that no one else has ever seen.

Insects are fascinating little animals. Most of them detect smells with their **antennae**; some taste with their feet. Some have no eyes; others have five eyes or more. Many are very strong; an ant, for example, can lift an object fifty times heavier than its own body weight.

▲ This insect is a type of giant weevil. Its antennae are positioned halfway down its long nose. At the end of this nose is the weevil's mouth. The female weevil uses her nose to drill a hole in which to lay her eggs.

◀ Leaf-cutter ants cut pieces of leaves from trees, plants, and shrubs. They carry the leaves back to their nest, holding them above their heads. Inside the nest, the ants chew the leaves into a pulp that is then left to rot. The ants feed on a fungus that grows on the rotting pulp.

Insects are great survivors, too. They can live in places too small for other animals, and they need little food. An insect's skeleton is on the outside of its body, which protects it against injury and prevents its body from losing moisture. Being able to fly makes it easier for some insects to find food and escape from enemies.

◀ This crab spider can disguise itself by changing the color of its body to match the flower it crawls on. Scientists call spiders arachnids because they are different from insects. They have eight legs, whereas insects have only six.

▼ The bright colors of this young grasshopper suggest that it might be a poisonous insect. This stops enemies such as spiders and beetles from approaching.

LIVING IN THE RAIN FOREST

Some tribes of people live deep in the rain forest, just as their ancestors have done for generations. Many of them farm using a method called slash-and-burn cultivation. First, they chop down trees to clear a space in the forest. They burn the trees and then plant seeds among the ashes. The crops grow quickly in the warm, moist ground. After a few years, the thin layer of soil is no

▼ Some houses, like this one in Indonesia, are built on stilts if the ground is swampy.

longer fertile, and crops do not grow well. The people move to another area and begin again.

Rain forest peoples also gather fruit and plants from the forest. They hunt animals using blowpipes, poisoned darts, bows and arrows, or spears.

Rain forest peoples build shelters that can be put up quickly when the group arrives in a new area.

◀ Embera Indians in Panama grinding manioc plant roots. The roots contain a poison called prussic acid, so they must be ground and washed before they can be eaten safely.

▼ A Penan man spears a fish in Sarawak, Malaysia.

CHANGING WAYS

The world's population has more than doubled in the last forty years and is steadily increasing at the rate of 155 people every minute. This dramatic rise causes enormous problems. People need somewhere to live and work, and they need food to eat. Huge areas of tropical rain forest have been cut down to provide areas for settlement and farming. In Brazil, for example, over one million people have been resettled in

In some tropical rain forests, **loggers** remove only certain trees or species of tree rather than simply cut down the whole area. But the heavy machinery used causes enormous damage. In Asia, for example, it is estimated that for every ten trees felled deliberately, another thirteen are seriously damaged.

cleared rain forest areas. Such efforts to **colonize** the rain forest often fail because the soil is too poor for crops to grow well.

With so many people in the world, the demand for goods like furniture, window frames, and doors made from **tropical hardwoods** such as mahogany and teak is very high. Tropical rain forests lie mostly in the poorer countries of the world, and these countries can make a lot of money selling timber to the world's richer countries. Other rain forest areas have been cut down to clear space for oil fields and mines.

▼ A section of the Amazon rain forest, cleared for settlement.

The effect of all these changes on the ways of life of many tropical rain forest peoples has been enormous. The destruction of the rain forests has made it more difficult for these peoples to survive by hunting and farming. Many of the animals and plants that they relied on for food have died out. Roads have been built through the forests, and settlers, miners, loggers, scientists, and even tourists now have access to areas that were once remote and unspoiled. These newcomers have brought diseases against which the rain forest peoples have no resistance.

▼ The Amazon rain forest in South America is the largest tropical rain forest in the world. Over 6,000 miles (9,700 km) of road now runs through this rain forest.

HOW ARE RAIN FORESTS USEFUL?

It is easy to guess that some pieces of furniture are made from the wood of a tropical rain forest tree. But did you know that golf balls, nail polish, deodorant, toothpaste, chewing gum, shampoo, and the glue on postage stamps are also made from or contain materials obtained from the world's tropical rain forests? Many foods have been developed from tropical rain forest plants. The medicine a

▼ A South American Indian collects latex to make rubber.

doctor prescribes for illness may contain plant extracts, and the soles of your favorite sneakers were made from the milky juice of a rubber tree.

Many of the foods we eat no longer come directly from the tropical rain forests, but are grown on large **plantations**.

Rain forest peoples have made medicines from plants for hundreds of years. It is only fairly recently, though, that scientists have discovered how useful tropical rain forest plants may be in producing lifesaving drugs that can be used to treat people all over the world. At least 1,400 plants found in tropical rain forests are now believed to offer possible treatments for cancer.

DECAYING LEAVES

The rain forest floor is covered with leaves, twigs, animal droppings, and the remains of dead animals. These waste materials break down and decay quickly in the moist heat, providing food for animals, insects, and plants. Try this experiment to see how leaves decompose.

You will need:
- Two plastic containers (one with a lid)
- Fresh, dry leaves
- Wet soil

1 Put some of the leaves in each container.

2 Add wet soil to one container, and pack it around the leaves. Put the lid on this container.

3 Look at the containers every few weeks. The ones in the wet soil will slowly begin to decay.

RAIN FORESTS IN DANGER

Many people believe that action must be taken now to save the world's tropical rain forests from total destruction. Scientists need to find ways of supplying timber without destroying entire forests. They need to develop ways of putting nutrients back into the soil left bare by forest clearance and organize **reforestation** plans.

Politicians and businesspeople need to cooperate with the native rain forest peoples, who know and understand the forests. People in rich countries need to reduce their demand for tropical hardwood and look for alternative materials.

Unless something is done quickly, all the possible benefits rain forests might bring to the world will be lost.

The world's climate may change, too. The destruction of the tropical rain forests has added to the growing amount of carbon dioxide in the atmosphere. Carbon dioxide and other gases **pollute** the air and are causing an alarming change in the world's climate. This change is known as **global warming** or the **greenhouse effect**.

▶ Slash-and-burn cultivation used to be limited to small areas of the rain forest. Today, however, huge areas are burned down by big companies.

◀ Every year, a certain area of the Amazon rain forest is flooded for six months or more. The waters can rise to a height of about 30 feet (9 m). Only the tops of the tallest trees remain above water. Others are completely underwater — but they go on growing! Normally, floods destroy trees, but in this area of the Amazon, when the flood waters go down, the trees have suffered no harm. This flooded forest is a unique habitat, with a huge variety of wildlife. It, too, is under threat of destruction.

RESCUE IN THE RAIN FOREST

The engine of the tiny plane coughed, spluttered, and stopped. O'Reilly and Jackson looked at each other in utter horror.

"Fasten your seat belts!" the pilot shouted as the plane began to lose height. He peered anxiously through the windshield, searching for a suitable landing spot. He could see nothing but trees. The rain forest stretched like a giant green carpet as far as the eye could see.

The jungle seemed to rush up toward them. Then, with a splintering crash, the plane plowed through the treetops, smashing through the branches until it finally came to a halt. It hung for a few

seconds, then slid, nose first, toward the ground. Then there was complete silence.

O'Reilly unfastened his seat belt and looked around. The plane was wedged above the ground at an incredible angle between two giant trees. A huge branch had ripped through the thin fuselage and was sticking into the cabin. O'Reilly became aware that his fellow passenger was groaning in pain. Hauling himself across the crazily angled floor, O'Reilly examined his companion carefully. Jackson's leg was broken.

O'Reilly spent several minutes finding the first aid kit and two reasonably straight tree branches for splints. He strapped the leg up as best he could and gave Jackson some painkillers. Then he groped his way to the cockpit. The pilot was unconscious.

O'Reilly returned to the cabin.

"The pilot's out cold, and the radio's broken," he explained. "It'll be hours before anyone misses us, let alone sends out a rescue party."

Jackson nodded stiffly.

"I'll go for help," continued O'Reilly. "I spotted a clearing not far away as we were coming down. I'll be as quick as I can."

Making Jackson as comfortable as he could, O'Reilly climbed out of the plane and grabbed hold of a vine to move down through the trees. Within minutes, his shirt was soaked with sweat from the sticky heat. Dust and dirt stuck to his damp skin. Branches scratched his arms and face and tore through his clothing as he forced his way downward.

When he reached the jungle floor, he found to his surprise that it was quite clear. A thick layer of leaves and animal droppings covered it, but only a few plants blocked his path. With one last glance at the plane, O'Reilly set out for the clearing.

In some places the trees nearly blotted out the sun, reducing the light to a green twilight. This made walking very difficult since he could not see fallen branches, roots, or ditches. He stumbled and tripped in these dark places. Swarms of insects buzzed around his face. O'Reilly brushed the insects away with his hand, but they returned moments later, thicker than ever.

All around, O'Reilly could hear the sounds of the rain forest. Birds and monkeys chattered loudly,

and branches creaked and swayed. From time to time, he caught glimpses of larger animals between the trees, but they all stayed out of his way.

O'Reilly stopped to rest when he reached a river. After hours of walking, he was exhausted. He

picked a piece of fruit off a nearby tree and ate it before going on, following the riverbank.

The bank was much harder to walk on than the forest floor. A tangle of roots and slimy mud covered it. Once, O'Reilly slipped and had to grab a branch to stop himself from falling into the water. As his foot splashed on the surface

of the water, he saw the long, low form of an alligator sliding into the river from the opposite bank. From then on, he walked more carefully.

At last he saw a flickering light through the trees. It was the campfire in a logging camp. With a last desperate burst of energy, O'Reilly staggered into the circle of firelight. The loggers started up in surprise at the sight of his scarecrow figure. O'Reilly stammered out his story.

Within minutes, the logging company's helicopter had taken off. In spite of O'Reilly's accurate directions, the rain forest seemed to have swallowed the wrecked plane. The helicopter crisscrossed the trees, its powerful searchlight probing the darkness below. It was over an hour before the helicopter finally hovered over the plane, while the crew winched up the injured pilot and passenger. A radio signal crackled the news to the logging camp, where O'Reilly sat staring into the firelight. When he heard that Jackson and the pilot were safe, he finally closed his eyes and fell into a deep sleep.

TRUE OR FALSE?

Which of the statements below are true and which are false?
If you have read this book carefully, you will know the answers.

1 The Amazon rain forest is the largest tropical rain forest in the world.

2 About a quarter of the world's species of plants and animals live in tropical rain forests.

3 All jungle animals are herbivores (plant-eaters).

4 Most tropical rain forest trees have branches only near the tops of their trunks.

5 Many tropical rain forest plants are used to cure illness and disease.

6 The climate in a tropical rain forest is cold and damp.

7 Epiphytes are a type of spider.

8 An ant can lift an object fifty times heavier than its own body weight.

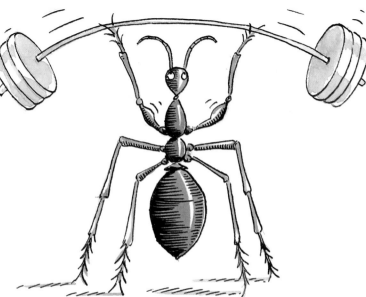

9 Many of the foods you eat have been developed from tropical rain forest plants.

10 Few tropical rain forest birds have brightly colored feathers.

11 The canopy forms a roof of leaves over the rain forest.

12 The waste materials on the rain forest floor provide food for animals, insects, trees, and plants.

GLOSSARY

Antennae are the parts of an insect's body used for touching and feeling other objects. Antennae are positioned on an insect's head.

Bromeliads are members of a large family of plants, most of which grow in the tropical rain forests of Central and South America. Most bromeliads are epiphytes, and have long, sword-shaped leaves.

Colonization means sending people from one area of a country to another

or from one country to another, so they can build homes and form a new town or settlement.

Epiphytes are plants that grow on other plants and take their food and water from the air.

Evergreens are trees that have green leaves all year round. Evergreens do shed their old leaves, but they form new ones first.

Extinction means dying out. A species of animal or plant becomes extinct when every one of its kind has died. Species usually become extinct because their habitat has been destroyed and they have lost their source of food.

Flora and fauna is a phrase used to refer to the plant and animal species found in a particular area.

Global warming and **greenhouse effect** are terms used to describe the warming of the earth by gases which have been released into the atmosphere. These gases trap heat, and so the earth warms up. Nobody is quite sure what the final effect will be, but if the earth continues to warm up, the ice at the poles will begin to melt. This will make the sea levels rise, and eventually a lot of land could disappear underwater.

Habitat is the term for the natural home of a plant or animal.

Lemurs are monkeylike animals that

are found on the island of Madagascar. Most lemurs live in trees. Some are active only at night.

Loggers are people who are hired to cut down trees.

Minerals are substances other than plants that can be dug from the ground.

Plantations are large areas of land used to grow a particular crop.

Pollute means to make something dirty or poisonous. Many factories, for example, dump garbage and chemicals into rivers and streams that poison the water and the fish that live there.

Pygmies are a group of native African people who live in the tropical rain forests of Zaire and neighboring areas. A pygmy's height usually ranges from 4 feet to 4 feet, 8 inches (1.2-1.4 m). Pygmies also live in some parts of Southeast Asia.

Reforestation means planting trees over a bare area of ground that was once covered by forest.

Species is the word used to describe a group of animals or plants that are alike in certain ways.

Tapir is a type of mammal that looks like a giant pig but is more closely related to the rhinoceros.

Tropical hardwoods are woods obtained from many tropical rain forest trees. Mahogany, ebony, teak, and rosewood are all tropical hardwoods.

INDEX